# If Not Now, Then When?

*Unveiling the Soul in Search of*
*Spiritual Freedom*

Robert E. Smith

Published And Distributed By
New Journey Publishing House
Memphis, Tennessee
Email: on.myway@hotmail.com

Packaging/Consulting
Professional Publishing House
1425 W. Manchester Ave. Ste B
Los Angeles, California 90047
323-750-3592
Email: professionalpublishinghouse@yahoo.com
www.Professionalpublishinghouse.com

Cover design: TWASolutions.com
First printing January 2024
979-8-218-34605-8
10987654321

*I extend my heartfelt dedication to my wife, Jacquelyn Thomas Smith, whose unwavering strength serves as a source of inspiration for my spiritual freedom and purposeful journey. Her frequent references to her mother's wisdom suggest that her mother played a significant role in shaping her character. In deep gratitude, I acknowledge the influence and guidance of my late mother-in-law, Annie Mae Thomas, may her soul rest in peace.*

# If Not Now, Then When?

*Unveiling the Soul in Search of*

*Spiritual Freedom*

# *Table of Contents*

# *Foreword*

In a world where conformity to religious norms often stifles the pursuit of spiritual truth, I have always dared to challenge the status quo. As a child, I sensed a dissonance between humanity's view of God and the expectations placed upon us. My spirit never settled for the accepted spiritual bondage of the majority; instead, I sought genuine spiritual freedom beyond the confines of man-made religious constructs.

Encountering Minister Robert Smith's manuscript was a revelation, as if he had penned the very thoughts that had long stirred within me. I found myself asking, "Did I write this? Is he echoing my sentiments?" Unable to set the manuscript aside, I was captivated by its freshness and the profound perspective it offered. Smith's literary work delves deep into the root of global unhappiness—the absence of meaning and purpose in people's lives.

True spiritual freedom, as eloquently expressed by the author, transcends materialism. It is the discovery of inner peace, purpose, and meaning that extends beyond life's external trappings. Smith's words resonate: "Spiritual freedom provides a sense of inner liberation that is not dependent on external circumstances." This book is an invaluable guide for those seeking a path to meaningful living, untethered from the confines of organized religion.

I wholeheartedly recommend "If Not Now, Then When? Unveiling the Soul in Search of Spiritual Freedom" to anyone on a quest for deeper meaning and a spiritual journey connected to the divine. Let this transformative work usher you into a new beginning, where the pursuit of spiritual truth leads to genuine freedom.

# Introduction

*If Not Now, Then When?: Unveiling the Soul in Search of Spiritual Freedom* is a thought-provoking exploration into the deep-rooted struggles and hesitations that often hinder us from fully embracing and expressing our spirituality.

In a world where materialism and skepticism prevail, this book aims to shed light on the various reasons behind the struggles and offer insights into how we overcome them. The profound human need for meaning and purpose is a fundamental aspect of our existence, deeply rooted in our spirituality. This need drives us to seek answers to existential questions that go beyond the physical realm and shape our understanding of the world and our place in it. Various philosophical and religious traditions, including the Bible, have explored these questions for millennia.

The journey toward spiritual freedom is a profound odyssey, a quest to unveil the depths of the soul and connect with something greater than oneself. While the destination promises liberation and enlightenment, the path is rife with struggles and hesitations that test the very core of our being.

The first and perhaps most fundamental struggle on the path to spiritual freedom is the fear of the unknown. Venturing beyond the boundaries of the material world, we step into uncharted territory. What lies there? What awaits us in the realm of the soul? These uncertainties can be paralyzing, causing hesitation as we stand at the threshold of spiritual exploration.

*Chapter 1*

## THE INNATE
## QUEST FOR MEANING AND PURPOSE

This chapter delves into the human need for meaning and purpose, which lies at the core of our spirituality. It explores the existential questions that arise within us, driving us beyond the physical realm. Through philosophical and psychological perspectives, it examines how this quest for meaning often clashes with societal pressures and norms.

Our materialistic society often keeps us tethered to the physical world, luring us with the illusion that we find happiness in possessions and achievements. The struggle lies in shedding these attachments. We hesitate to relinquish the familiar comforts of materialism, fearing the pursuit of spiritual freedom may mean sacrificing the security and pleasures to which we've grown accustomed

The pursuit of meaning and purpose is an intrinsic facet of the human experience, closely intertwined with our spirituality. It serves as a guiding light that illuminates our life's path, lending depth and significance to our actions. This innate need transcends cultural, religious, and geographic boundaries, underscoring its relevance.

Throughout human history, individuals and societies have grappled with questions such as: Why are we here? What is the purpose of life? What happens after we die? These questions are not only intellectual pursuits but also deeply spiritual ones, as they touch on the core of our existence. Many people turn to religion and philosophy in their quest for answers.

The Bible, one of the most influential texts in human history, provides numerous references that address the quest for meaning and purpose. For instance, in the Book of Ecclesiastes, King Solomon reflects on the futility of worldly pursuits and ultimately concludes that *"Fear God and keep his commandments, for this is the whole duty of man"* (Ecclesiastes 12:13). This suggests that a sense of purpose is tied intricately to the reverence of God.

At the heart of the human need for meaning and purpose lies our spirituality. Regardless of one's religious affiliation or belief, humans always seek a connection with something greater than themselves. This quest for a deeper connection, whether with a divine being (God) the universe, or the transcendent, is an integral part of our spiritual journey.

This need for meaning and purpose is a powerful intrinsic motivator. It gives individuals a sense of direction and a reason to strive for more in life. It shapes our decisions, values, and goals, guiding us towards actions and experiences that align with our sense of purpose.

## *Transcending Materialism Into Spiritual Freedom*

While our physical needs are essential, our innate spirituality prompts us to consider the deeper, intangible aspects of our humanity, such as the quest for wisdom, love, and spiritual fulfillment. Many of us look to spirituality and religious beliefs as a source of guidance and meaning, often experiencing a sense of transcendence that goes beyond the limitations of the physical world.

Materialism, in the philosophical and cultural sense, is the excessive focus on material wealth and possessions as the primary source of meaning and happiness. It often leads to a shallow and unsatisfying existence, devoid of deeper spiritual fulfillment.

Transcending materialism involves moving beyond this narrow worldview and recognizing the transformative relationship it can have with spiritual freedom. Recognizing that the focus of materialism, as a philosophy of life, is based on the belief that accumulating wealth, possessions, and external achievements leads to happiness and fulfillment. However, this perspective often leads to a sense of emptiness and discontent, as material possessions alone cannot satisfy the deeper yearnings of the human spirit.

It becomes essential to recognize the limitations of materialism and its inability to provide lasting happiness. Transcending materialism involves a call for transcendence—a journey beyond the superficial and materialistic pursuits dominating our lives. It requires a shift in perspective, a reevaluation of what truly matters, and a recognition of the importance of inner growth and spiritual fulfillment.

## *Embracing Spiritual Freedom*

Spiritual freedom, in contrast to materialism, is about finding inner peace, purpose, and meaning that goes beyond the external trappings of life. It is the freedom to explore one's spirituality, connect with deeper truths, and live in alignment with one's values and beliefs. Spiritual freedom provides a sense of inner liberation that is not dependent on external circumstances.

Transcending materialism often involves practices like mindfulness and meditation. These practices encourage us to be fully present in the moment, fostering a deeper connection between ourselves and the world around us. Through mindfulness, we can cultivate spiritual freedom by breaking free from the constant desire for more material possessions and appreciating the richness of the present moment.

Practicing gratitude and contentment are powerful tools for transcending materialism. When we recognize and appreciate the blessings in our lives, we shift our focus from what we lack to what we already have. This shift can lead to a profound sense of contentment and spiritual freedom, as we are no longer driven by the relentless pursuit of external wealth.

Engaging in acts of service and showing compassion towards others can also be transformative in transcending materialism. When we shift our focus from accumulating for ourselves to giving and helping others, we often experience a deep sense of purpose and fulfillment. This shift in perspective aligns with spiritual freedom, as it emphasizes the interconnectedness of all beings.

Transcending materialism also involves a commitment to inner growth and self-reflection. This process allows us to explore our values, beliefs, and spiritual dimensions. It encourages a deeper understanding of oneself and one's place in the universe, ultimately leading to a greater sense of spiritual freedom.

Many spiritual traditions and religions emphasize the importance of transcending materialism. For example, Buddhism teaches the impermanence of material possessions and pursuing inner enlightenment. Christianity teaches that one cannot serve both God and wealth, highlighting the need to prioritize spiritual values over material gain. These teachings offer guidance and wisdom on the transformative journey from materialism to spiritual freedom.

Transcending materialism is a transformative journey that opens the door to spiritual freedom. It involves recognizing the limitations of material pursuits, embracing practices that foster mindfulness, gratitude, service, and inner growth, and drawing wisdom from spiritual traditions. Through this process, we can experience a profound shift in our lives, finding true meaning and fulfillment that transcends the superficial and materialistic aspects of existence. Spiritual freedom becomes the guiding force, leading us towards a deeper understanding of ourselves, our purpose, and our connection to our Lord.

*Chapter 2*

CONFLICT WITH
SOCIETAL PRESSURES AND NORMS

The quest for meaning and purpose can conflict with societal pressures and norms. In many societies, there are expectations about what a meaningful and purposeful life should look like, often revolving around material success, social status, or conformity to certain cultural values. These societal pressures can create tension for those of us who are on a spiritual or philosophical quest for deeper meaning. Society often places expectations upon us, prescribing norms and values that may not align with our spiritual journey. The struggle here is the tension between conforming to societal pressures and pursuing spiritual freedom. Fear of social rejection or isolation can be a powerful deterrent. The ego, that persistent sense of self, resists the dissolution that spiritual freedom implies. It clings to identity, status, and worldly desires, making it challenging to break free. The ego hesitates to relinquish control, fearing its own annihilation in the process.

## *The Intersection of Spirituality and Societal Pressures*

Finding a balance between the quest for meaning and societal pressures is a profound challenge. Many of us must navigate this tension, often undergoing periods of personal growth and transformation. We may need to question and reevaluate our values, goals, and priorities, which can lead to a deeper understanding of ourselves and our purpose.

In Christianity, the search for meaning and purpose often centers on the belief in a divine plan. Christians believe that we all have a unique role within God's grand design, finding ultimate purpose and fulfillment in aligning our lives with this divine purpose.

Doubt is a formidable adversary on the path to spiritual freedom. It creeps in, questioning the validity of our experiences and the authenticity of our spiritual pursuits.

21

Skepticism can breed hesitancy, making us question whether our efforts are worthwhile or mere flights of imagination.

*"Trust in the Lord with all your heart and lean not on your own understanding; in all your ways submit to him, and he will make your path straight."*
—Proverbs 3:5-6

Society always values conformity and adherence to established norms. However, the quest for meaning may lead us to embrace our unique path, which can challenge societal expectations. This tension between conformity and authenticity can be emotionally and psychologically taxing.

Societal pressures often prioritize material success, such as wealth and career achievement. Yet, many of us find that true fulfillment comes from pursuing a meaningful life, which may not align with the relentless pursuit of material goals. To avoid rejection, we often conform to societal norms and expectations. This conformity can manifest in various ways, from conforming to fashion trends to adopting certain beliefs and values.

Conformity can provide a sense of safety and acceptance

within a group. The fear of rejection can have a significant impact on self-esteem. Rejection, whether real or perceived, can bruise our self-worth and lead to feelings of inadequacy. The fear of experiencing these emotions can be so intense that it influences our actions, causing us to avoid situations where rejection is possible.

While social norms are essential for maintaining order and cohesion in society, social dogma can limit our freedom and stifle creativity. It discourages questioning or challenging established beliefs and practices. The intersection of spirituality and societal pressure is a complex and often challenging terrain we must navigate in our quest for meaning, purpose, and personal growth. Spirituality, which involves a deep connection with the self, the divine, or a higher purpose, can come into conflict with the expectations, norms, and pressures imposed by society. Social dogma creates a climate to resist or even condemn deviations from the norm. This fear of deviation can be a powerful force in preventing us from pursuing our unique paths, choices, or beliefs.

*"When I'm afraid I put my trust in you. In God whose words I praise—in God I trust and am not afraid. What can mere mortals do to me?"*

— Psalms: 56: 3-4

*"We should not worry about what man thinks about us or says about us, for only God can give you salvation or take salvation away."*

#hashtagunveilingthesoul#

Breaking free from the cycle of fear of rejection and social dogma can be a transformative journey, requiring self-awareness and encouraging us to embark on a journey of self-discovery and authenticity. It prompts us to explore our inner selves, beliefs, and values, and to live in alignment with these principles. However, societal pressure can act as a counterforce, urging us to conform to established norms and expectations. This tension between authenticity and conformity is a central theme in the intersection of spirituality and societal pressure.

Overcoming these fears and societal pressures allows us to embrace authenticity. Authenticity is the path to true self-discovery and fulfillment, as it involves living in alignment with one's values, beliefs, and passions. Societal pressure exerts a powerful influence on us to conform to prevailing standards and conventions. This pressure can manifest in various ways, including conformity to cultural norms, religious doctrines, economic aspirations, and social expectations. Conformity often discourages us from questioning or challenging the status quo, potentially stifling our spiritual growth and self-exploration.

Many spiritual journeys involve personal beliefs and experiences that may not align with mainstream societal narratives. We may hesitate to express or explore these beliefs because of fear of rejection, ridicule, or isolation. The suppression of these beliefs can hinder spiritual development and authenticity.

Spirituality often revolves around the search for meaning and purpose in life. It encourages us to explore profound questions about existence, morality, and the nature of reality. However, societal pressure can prioritize material success, external validation, and achievement over these existential inquiries. This clash can leave us feeling torn between our spiritual quest and societal demands.

Navigating the intersection of spirituality and societal pressure requires a nuanced approach. Recognizing the influence of societal pressure and its impact on one's beliefs and actions is the first step toward navigating this intersection. It encourages questioning and introspection, enabling individuals to discern which aspects of societal pressure align with their spiritual values and which do not. Authenticity is paramount. This involves living in alignment with one's spiritual values and beliefs, even when it requires challenging societal expectations.

The intersection of spirituality and societal pressure is a multifaceted terrain where individuals must navigate the delicate balance between authenticity and conformity, personal growth, and societal expectations. While societal pressure can pose challenges to spiritual development, it is possible to find harmony by fostering self-awareness, critical thinking, and authenticity. Ultimately, the journey toward spiritual fulfillment requires us to chart our own path, honoring our beliefs and values while navigating the complex dynamics of the societies in which they live.

*Chapter 3*

## FEAR OF REJECTION AND
## SOCIAL STIGMA

Delving into the intricacies of human psychology, this chapter examines the fear of rejection and the social stigma that often accompanies open expressions of spirituality. It explores how societal prejudices, stereotypes, and misconceptions surrounding spirituality can lead to hesitations and inhibitions.

The fear of rejection and social stigma can cast a long shadow over the open expression of spirituality. As we seek to share our deepest spiritual beliefs, practices, and experiences with others, we often grapple with these two powerful forces that can hinder our authentic ability to express and embrace our spiritual journey.

The open expression of spirituality often requires us to share deeply personal experiences and beliefs. Whether it's discussing mystical encounters, un conventional practices, or alternative worldviews, the fear of rejection can be a formidable obstacle. The vulnerability of exposing one's spiritual journey to potential ridicule or rejection can be paralyzing.

## *Overcoming the Fear of Rejection*

*"If anyone will not welcome you or listen to your words, leave that home or town and shake the dust off your feet. Truly I tell you, it will be more bearable for Sodom and Gomorrah on the Day of Judgment than for that town."*
— Matthew 10:14-15 (NIV)

This scripture reminds us that not everyone will be receptive to our spiritual message. It encourages us to share our beliefs, but also to be prepared for rejection.

Embracing one's own spiritual journey and finding self-acceptance can be a powerful antidote to the fear of rejection. When we are secure in our beliefs and experiences, the opinions of others may hold less sway.

The fear of rejection is a powerful and deeply rooted

human emotion that can have a significant impact on one's pursuit of spiritual freedom. It is a fear that stems from our innate need for social acceptance and belonging, making it a complex and often paralyzing force in our lives.

In the context of spiritual freedom, the fear of rejection can manifest in various ways, hindering us from fully expressing and embracing our spiritual beliefs and practices. Spiritual freedom often involves breaking away from societal norms and expectations. However, the fear of rejection can cause hesitation, as we worry about not conforming to established norms and being perceived as different or deviant. This fear can stifle spiritual exploration and expression, trapping us in a cycle of conformity to societal expectations. The fear of rejection becomes particularly pronounced when we contemplate sharing our deeply personal and spiritual experiences with others. This fear can lead us to keep our spiritual experiences hidden, depriving us of the opportunity to connect with like-minded individuals and deepen our spiritual journey.

*"If the world hates you, keep in mind that it hated me first."*
—John 15:18 (NIV)

This scripture reminds us that even Jesus, a central figure in Christianity, faced rejection and stigma. It serves as a reminder that spiritual individuals may encounter resistance from the world.

Connecting with like-minded individuals or spiritual communities can provide a sense of belonging and acceptance. Sharing one's spiritual journey within such communities can mitigate the fear of rejection from those who do not share the same beliefs. It offers a safe space for open expression and growth.

It takes courage to embrace one's uniqueness and spiritual path, even when it deviates from societal norms. Recognizing that spiritual freedom often lies outside the boundaries of conformity can empower us to confront our fear of rejection and boldly walk our chosen path. Many spiritual traditions and teachings offer guidance on facing the fear of rejection.

*"For the Spirit God gave us does not make us timid, but gives us power, love, and self-discipline."*
—2 Timothy 1:7 (NIV)

This scripture reminds us that the divine presence within us can provide the strength to overcome fear and embrace our spiritual freedom with courage and love.

Overcoming the fear of rejection related to spiritual freedom is a profound and liberating journey that allows us to embrace our spirituality authentically and without reservation. This fear can be a significant obstacle to one's spiritual growth and self-discovery, but individuals can navigate this challenge with courage and self-compassion.

Recognize that spirituality is a deeply personal and individual journey. There is no one-size-fits-all approach to spirituality, and each person's path is unique. Embrace your beliefs, practices, and experiences as valid and valuable, even if they differ from those around you.

Examine and challenge negative beliefs that fuel the fear of rejection. Often, individuals root these beliefs in irrational fears and limiting self-perceptions. Cognitive-behavioral techniques can help you reframe these beliefs and replace them with more empowering and accurate thoughts.

*"Do not be conformed to this world, but be transformed by the renewal of your mind."*

—Romans 12:2

This verse encourages believers to challenge worldly beliefs and renew their thinking.

Intimately tied to authenticity, spiritual freedom is the freedom to be true to oneself and to explore one's beliefs and experiences without fear of rejection or judgment. Embracing authenticity in one's spiritual journey is a liberating and transformative process. It involves living in alignment with one's values, beliefs, and passions, regardless of external pressures.

Remember that your spirituality is a deeply personal and valid aspect of your identity, deserving of respect and acceptance, both from yourself and from the world around you.

*Chapter 4*

CONFRONTING THE ULTIMATE
BATTLE FOR SPIRITUAL FREEDOM

C onfronting the ultimate battle is a profound and deeply
personal journey that goes to the core of one's beliefs,
values, and connection to the divine. This battle often involves
overcoming inner and outer obstacles, facing doubts and
challenges, and seeking a higher state of consciousness or
liberation.

Just as with any significant endeavor in life, the quest for
spiritual freedom requires a courageous confrontation with
various inner and outer forces that seek to obstruct or divert
this sacred path.

## *Inner Struggles*

The ultimate battle for spiritual freedom often involves internal struggles. The battle within, often described as the struggle of the soul, is a central aspect of the spiritual journey towards greater freedom, self-realization, and enlightenment. This inner battle encompasses various challenges and adversaries that we encounter as we seek to transcend limitations and expand our spiritual consciousness. These can include doubts about one's faith, the challenge of overcoming one's desires, and pursuing higher states of spiritual consciousness. The spiritual journey often requires us to confront our inner demons—deep-seated fears, insecurities, traumas, and unresolved emotional baggage. This inner battle can be arduous and emotionally challenging.

The apostle Paul writes about the inner struggle in Romans 7:15, stating, *"I do not understand what I do. For what I want to do I do not, but what I hate I do."*

This reflects the inner conflict, deep-seated fears, insecurities, traumas, and unresolved emotional baggage that we carry within us. These inner adversaries can cast a shadow over pursuing spiritual freedom, causing emotional turmoil and inner conflicts. The battle within is often a deeply personal one, requiring us to face our inner demons with courage and compassion to heal and find liberation.

Attachment to worldly possessions, relationships, and desires can be a formidable obstacle on the path to spiritual freedom. The battle within centers on learning to detach from these attachments, recognizing their impermanence, and embracing a state of contentment and inner peace that is not dependent on external factors.

Self-awareness is a powerful ally in the battle within. It involves recognizing and understanding one's inner struggles, doubts, and egoist tendencies. Through self-awareness, we can disentangle ourselves from the ego's grip and confront our inner adversaries with clarity. Building inner strength through spiritual practices, such as meditation and prayer, can help us navigate the battle within. These practices cultivate resilience, emotional stability, and a deeper connection to one's spiritual essence. Embracing authenticity is crucial to the battle within. Authenticity involves living in alignment with one's core values, beliefs, and spiritual principles, even when it requires confronting inner demons or facing external challenges.

*"The righteous cry out, and the Lord hears them; he delivers them from all their troubles. The Lord is close to the brokenhearted and saves those who are crushed in spirit."*
— Psalm 34:17-18 (NIV)

This scripture reminds us that in the battle within, seeking divine guidance and assistance can provide strength and solace in times of inner turmoil.

The battle within is an integral part of the spiritual journey towards greater freedom and self-realization. Confronting inner adversaries, such as the ego, doubt, inner demons, and attachment, is a courageous and transformative process. It requires self-awareness, inner strength, and a commitment to authenticity.

Ultimately, the battle within leads to the liberation of the soul, allowing us to transcend limitations, attain greater spiritual freedom, and connect with the boundless potential of our inner selves.

## The Battle Without

The battle without, which is often referred to as the external challenges faced on the path to spiritual freedom, encompasses the various obstacles and adversities that we encounter in the external world as we seek to deepen our spiritual understanding and attain greater freedom. These external challenges can often test one's resolve and commitment to our spiritual journey.

Society exerts immense pressure on us to conform to established norms and expectations. This can be challenging, particularly for those on a spiritual path that may deviate from societal conventions. The battle lies in resisting conformity and staying true to one's beliefs and practices. The materialistic culture that surrounds us can distract and deter us from pursuing spiritual freedom. The battle is in discerning what truly matters amidst the allure of material possessions and worldly success. External skepticism or criticism of one's spiritual beliefs and experiences can be disheartening. The battle is in maintaining the faith and conviction to continue the journey, even in the face of external resistance.

One of the most significant external challenges on the journey to spiritual freedom is the pressure to conform to societal norms and expectations. Society often considers and dictates what is acceptable, and deviation from these norms, especially in the realm of spirituality, can lead to resistance, ridicule, or ostracism. The battle without involves resisting conformity and staying true to one's spiritual beliefs and practices, even in the face of societal pressures.

The materialistic culture that pervades modern society can be a potent adversary on the spiritual path. The pursuit of material wealth, possessions, and external success often takes precedence over pursuing inner peace and spiritual growth. The battle without centers on discerning what truly matters amid the allure of material possessions and worldly achievements. External skepticism or criticism of one's spiritual beliefs and experiences can be challenging to navigate. Friends, family members, or colleagues may question or dismiss one's spiritual journey, which can be disheartening. The battle without requires us to maintain faith and conviction, even in the face of external resistance.

Developing self-confidence and a strong sense of self are crucial in navigating the battle without. Believing in one's spiritual path and the validity of one's experiences can help withstand external pressures. It takes courage to embrace one's uniqueness and spiritual path, even when it deviates from societal norms. The battle without involves acknowledging that spiritual freedom often exists outside the boundaries of conformity and bravely walking that chosen path.

*"Do not conform to the pattern of this world, but be transformed by the renewing of your mind. Then you will be able to test and approve what God's will is—his good, pleasing, and perfect will."*

— Romans 12:2 (NIV)

This scripture encourages individuals to resist conformity to worldly patterns and seek transformation through spiritual renewal, even in the face of external challenges.

The battle without, which are external challenges such as societal conformity, materialism, external skepticism, and social stigma, is an integral part of the spiritual journey towards greater freedom and self-realization. Confronting these external adversaries requires self-confidence, a supportive community, courage, and a commitment to education and advocacy.

Ultimately, the battle without leads to the realization that spiritual freedom is a deeply personal and valid path, even in the face of external pressures. It allows us to transcend external limitations, attain greater spiritual freedom, and connect with the profound potential of our inner selves.

Developing self-confidence and a strong sense of self are crucial in navigating the battle without. Believing in one's spiritual path and the validity of one's experiences can help withstand external pressures.

*"So we say with confidence, 'The Lord is my helper; I will not be afraid. What can mere mortals do to me?'"*

—Hebrews 13:6 (NIV)

Faith can provide us with the strength to overcome the fear of rejection and social stigma. Belief in a higher power and a divine purpose can empower us to stand firm in our spirituality, regardless of external pressures.

*Chapter 5*

## COURAGE TO BE DIFFERENT

It takes courage to embrace one's uniqueness and spiritual path, even when it deviates from societal norms. The battle without involves acknowledging that spiritual freedom often exists outside the boundaries of conformity and bravely walking that chosen path. In pursuing spiritual freedom, we often find ourselves faced with the need for courage—to stand apart from societal norms and expectations, to embrace our unique spiritual path, and to be different in a world that often values conformity. Courage to be different is a vital aspect of the spiritual journey, for it allows us to be authentic in expressing our beliefs and experiences while navigating the complexities of external pressures.

Spiritual freedom often involves breaking away from societal norms and expectations. It may require us to explore unconventional beliefs, practices, or worldviews. Breaking away from the status quo can provoke resistance, skepticism, or even condemnation from others.

> *"Have I not commanded you? Be strong and courageous.*
> *Do not be afraid; do not be discouraged, for the Lord*
> *your God will be with you wherever you go."*
> —Joshua 1:9 (NIV)

This scripture emphasizes the divine support available to those who exhibit courage, reminding us we need not fear when we align ourselves with our spiritual purpose.

## *The Call for Courage*

Embracing one's uniqueness and having the courage to be different begins with self-acceptance. We must recognize the value and validity of our spiritual paths and experiences.

Courage is a virtue that transcends cultural, geographical, and temporal boundaries. It is the quality that enables us to confront adversity, uncertainty, and fear with strength and determination. Courage is not the absence of fear, but the willingness to act despite it by being different and deviating from societal norms, maintaining faith and spiritual practices with resilience, trusting in the journey's ultimate purpose and significance, and embracing one's unique beliefs and experiences. Courageously exploring one's spiritual beliefs, practices, and experiences, even in the face of skepticism or criticism.

*"Spiritual freedom is not something that is inherent or that comes naturally, it is something we can activate by faith."*
#hashtagunveilingthesoul#

Some people can't grasp the practicality of God's words because they need to see the outcome of something tangible before they will believe in it. However, God's words and His plan are based solely on faith. Even though they can see the world as we know it, slowly decaying before their eyes (literally and physically), they waiver in the opportunity to embrace the light. I believe that light represents hope and serves as the source of our existence. It's like the pilot light of life, patiently waiting for us to intensify it so that we can allow our inner light, often seen as the holy spirit, to radiate from within us. However, for this to occur, we need to release our worldly thoughts and behaviors and place our trust in the source of our existence. This is where faith takes over, and the more we trust, the stronger our faith becomes.

*"God honors faith because faith honors God."*
#hashtagunveilingthesoul#

The courage to be different is an essential quality for those on the path to spiritual freedom. It empowers us to break free from conformity's constraints, express our spirituality authentically, and navigate the complexities of external pressures. Courage is not just a human attribute; it is also a divine command and a source of strength for those who seek spiritual liberation. Ultimately, embracing one's uniqueness and having the courage to be different are transformative acts that lead to a deeper connection with the self, a greater understanding of one's spiritual purpose, and the realization of true spiritual freedom.

*"Trust in the Lord with all your heart and lean not on*
*your own understanding; in all your ways submit to*
*him, and he will make your paths straight."*
—Proverbs 3:5-6 (NIV)

This scripture emphasizes the courage to trust in a higher power and submit to a divine path, even when it is beyond human comprehension.

The call to courage is an ever-present, universal invitation that defines the essence of the human spirit. It encourages us to face personal challenges with resilience, navigate relationships with vulnerability and authenticity, drive societal change with conviction and empathy, and embrace spiritual freedom with nonconformity and faith. In heeding this call, we embark on a journey of self-discovery, growth, and transformation, ultimately realizing that courage is not merely a virtue—it is a guiding force that empowers us to lead lives of purpose, authenticity, and meaning.

# Chapter 6

## THE NEED FOR EVIDENCE
## ON THE PATH TO SPIRITUAL FREEDOM

The pursuit of spiritual freedom is a deeply personal journey that often involves beliefs and experiences beyond empirical evidence. In this context, the need for evidence takes on a nuanced dimension where faith and reason intersect. While faith plays a central role in matters of spirituality, there is a need for a balance that allows us to navigate our journey with discernment and authenticity. Faith is a foundational concept in many spiritual traditions, including Christianity. Often described as the belief in the unseen or the unproven, in matters of spirituality, faith involves trust in a higher power, the validity of spiritual experiences, and the existence of a divine realm. It provides the spiritual seeker with a sense of purpose, meaning, and connection to something greater than themselves.

*"Now faith is confidence in what we hope for and assurance about what we do not see."*
—Hebrews 11:1 (NIV)

This verse from the Book of Hebrews highlights the essence of faith as confidence in the unseen. It acknowledges that faith often involves belief in things that are not empirically evident.

## *The Need for Evidence*

While faith is essential in spirituality, the need for evidence remains relevant. Evidence in this context may not always be empirical or tangible, but it can take various forms. Many of us have personal spiritual experiences that provide a form of evidence for us. These experiences may include moments of divine presence, inner transformation, or deep spiritual insights. Spiritual traditions often have historical records, scriptures, and teachings that serve as evidence of the spiritual journey of others. For Christians, the Bible is a primary source of such evidence. The shared experiences and traditions within spiritual communities can also serve as a form of evidence. These traditions often contain rituals, practices, and narratives that reinforce spiritual beliefs.

> *"Then Jesus told him, 'Because you have seen me, you have believed; blessed are those who have not seen and yet have believed.'"*
> —John 20:29 (NIV)

In this passage, Jesus speaks to the importance of belief without direct empirical evidence. He acknowledges the blessedness of those who have faith without requiring tangible proof.

## *Navigating the Balance*

While faith is essential, discernment plays a crucial role in pursuing spiritual freedom. Discernment involves critically evaluating one's beliefs and experiences to ensure they align with one's understanding of spirituality. Being open to spiritual experiences and insights is essential. While these experiences may not always have empirical evidence, they can be deeply transformative and meaningful on a personal level. Recognizing that different individuals and spiritual traditions may have varying forms of evidence and beliefs is crucial. Respect for diversity allows for a more inclusive and tolerant approach to spirituality. Encouraging personal exploration and reflection allows us to deepen our understanding of our spiritual beliefs and experiences. It fosters a sense of authenticity and ownership of one's spiritual journey.

Spiritual freedom involves the liberation of the soul from worldly constraints and a deep connection with the divine. While faith is the cornerstone of this journey, the need for evidence, whether personal, historical, or communal, provides us with a sense of validation and assurance on our path. The need for evidence on the path to spiritual freedom is a complex interplay between faith and reason. It involves the recognition that, while faith is the foundation of spirituality, evidence in various forms can support and validate one's beliefs and experiences. As we navigate this balance, we embark on a profound journey of self-discovery, connection with the divine, and the attainment of spiritual freedom.

Ultimately, pursuing spiritual freedom is a deeply personal and transformative quest that requires both faith and a discerning heart. Faith is not merely a belief; it's a steadfast trust, an unwavering assurance that keeps us grounded in the face of adversity. Just as a ship's anchor keeps it secure amidst raging waters, faith anchors our souls in turbulent times. This anchoring power of faith provides stability in our ever-changing lives.

> *"The testing of your faith produces perseverance. Let perseverance finish its work so that you may be mature and complete, not lacking anything."*
> — James 1:3-4 (NIV)

Faith strengthens us in adversity, enabling personal growth and spiritual maturity. Faith is the anchor that steadies our souls, strengthens us in adversity, guides us in darkness, and fuels our hope. As we face life's tempests, let us remember these words.

*The Need For Evidence On the Path to Spiritual Freedom*

*"Now faith is confidence in what we hope for and assurance about what we do not see."*

—Hebrews 11:1 (NIV)


*"May our faith be a steadfast anchor in our journey, providing the assurance and hope we need to overcome life's trials."*

—Hebrews 6:19

*Chapter 7*

## LIVNIG WITH PURPOSE

L et's embark on a profound journey into the essence of living with purpose—a journey that transcends the mere act of existing and invites us to embrace a life of meaning, fulfillment, and spiritual connection. Life is a magnificent gift, yet it becomes truly meaningful when we discover our purpose. Purpose gives our existence direction and ignites our passion. It beckons us to move beyond the mundane and embrace a life filled with significance.

*"There is a time for everything, and a season for every activity under the heavens."*
— In Ecclesiastes 3:1 (NIV)

Living With Purpose

This verse reminds us that life has seasons, and each season can be an opportunity to discover and live out our purpose.

Purpose often lies in serving others. In Matthew 20:28 (NIV), we find, "just as the Son of Man did not come to be served, but to serve, and to give his life as a ransom for many." Serving others allows us to make a meaningful impact on the lives of those around us. Serving others in a spiritual context is not only an outward expression of love and compassion, but also a powerful means of personal transformation. When we serve selflessly, we transcend our ego-driven desires and connect with our higher selves. This transformation aligns with the spiritual journey of becoming more compassionate, empathetic, and loving beings. Serving others encourages humility and gratitude. It reminds us of our interconnectedness and the importance of recognizing the blessings in our lives. Often considered a spiritual practice in itself, gratitude reinforces the idea that our service is an expression of thankfulness for what we have received.

*"The King will reply, 'Truly I tell you, whatever you did for one of the least of these brothers and sisters of mine, you did for me.'"*
— Matthew 25:40 (NIV)

This verse from the New Testament underscores the spiritual significance of serving others. It teaches that acts of service to fellow human beings are, in essence, acts of service to the divine. Living with purpose often involves leaving a positive legacy.

In 2 Timothy 4:7 (NIV), the Apostle Paul reflects on his life, saying, *"I have fought the good fight, I have finished the race, I have kept the faith."*

Leaving a legacy requires steadfastness in our purpose.

## *Hope For the Future*

Faith is the anchor that keeps hope alive. Let's explore the profound concept of hope for the future from a spiritual perspective. Amid life's challenges and uncertainties, hope serves as a guiding light, providing solace, strength, and purpose. Let us delve into the significance of hope in our spiritual journey and the wisdom offered by various spiritual traditions.

Romans 15:13 (NIV) reminds us, *"May the God of hope fill you with all joy and peace as you trust in him, so that you may overflow with hope by the power of the Holy Spirit."*

Faith assures us that, despite life's challenges, a brighter future awaits. Hope is more than just wishful thinking; it is a deep and unwavering trust in the possibility of positive outcomes, even in the face of adversity. From a spiritual perspective, hope transcends the material realm, inviting us to connect with a higher power and a greater purpose. Hope fosters compassion and empathy and encourages us to see the potential for goodness in others and to extend a helping hand, aligning with the teachings of many spiritual traditions that emphasize love and service. It provides inner peace and tranquility, even amid life's storms. It reminds us that we are not alone in our journey, and there is a higher purpose guiding our lives. Hope enables us to face adversity with resilience and determination. It empowers us to see challenges as opportunities for growth and transformation.

*"Consider it pure joy, my brothers and sisters, whenever you face trials of many kinds because you know that the testing of your faith produces perseverance."*

—James 1:2-3 (NIV)

In the tapestry of life, there are moments when events unfold effortlessly, like a well-choreographed dance, and there are times when progress seems stalled, leaving us in a state of uncertainty. It's during these moments of seeming stagnation when trusting in divine timing—a fundamental concept in many spiritual and religious traditions—is challenging. From a spiritual perspective, trusting divine timing is an act of patience, faith, and surrender, acknowledging there is a divine power at work guiding our lives. Divine timing is the belief that there is a higher plan or purpose governing the unfolding of events in our lives. It posits that certain events, circumstances, and opportunities align precisely with our highest good and spiritual growth. This concept transcends the human desire for immediate results and invites us to surrender to a higher wisdom.

In a fast-paced world, impatience can easily take hold. The desire for instant gratification, immediate success, and swift solutions can lead to frustration and anxiety when things don't go as planned. However, the spiritual perspective on divine timing invites us to embrace patience as a virtue.

Patience is more than just waiting; it is an active practice of maintaining inner calm and trust while awaiting outcomes.

It allows us to cultivate resilience and emotional stability in the face of life's uncertainties.

Trusting divine timing requires us to accept uncertainty as an inherent part of life. Uncertainty can be an opportunity for personal growth, humility, and strengthening our faith. When we release the need to control outcomes and trust in a higher plan, we experience a profound sense of peace and serenity. We no longer carry the burden of worry and anxiety about the future. Trusting divine timing deepens our faith in a higher power or universal intelligence. It reinforces the belief that there is a purpose and order to the universe, even when circumstances seem unclear. Moments of waiting and uncertainty are often opportunities for significant spiritual growth. They challenge us to develop qualities such as patience, humility, and resilience, which are integral to our spiritual journey.

Trusting divine timing is a profound spiritual perspective that invites us to embrace patience, faith, and surrender in the face of life's uncertainties. It reminds us that there is a higher plan at work that's guiding our journey toward growth and fulfillment. As we navigate the complexities of life, let us find solace and strength in the wisdom of trusting divine timing, knowing that it leads us toward a future filled with purpose and grace.

### *Humility and Gratitude*

Pursuing spiritual freedom, the qualities of humility and gratitude stand as essential pillars. These virtues not only guide us toward a deeper connection with the divine but also pave the way for a liberated and enriched soul. Humility is the quality of having a modest and unpretentious view of oneself. It involves recognizing our limitations, imperfections, and interconnectedness with all of creation. In many spiritual traditions, humility is the foundation of spiritual growth.

*"But he gives us more grace. That is why Scripture says: 'God opposes the proud but shows favor to the humble."*
— James 4:6 (NIV)

This verse from the Book of James emphasizes the divine preference for the humble. It underscores that humility opens the door to God's grace and favor, facilitating our spiritual journey.

Humility fosters openness to divine guidance. When we recognize our limited understanding, we become receptive to the wisdom and direction of the creator. It also emphasizes our interconnectedness with all beings. This awareness encourages compassion and empathy, which are vital for spiritual growth and liberation. Pursuing spiritual freedom, humility and gratitude is not mere virtues but transformative forces. They lead us away from the ego's confines, opening our hearts to divine guidance and interconnectedness with all of creation. These qualities shift our perspective from scarcity to abundance, cultivating joy and deepening our faith. Embrace humility and gratitude, liberate our souls, and we find ourselves on a path of profound spiritual freedom, guided by the wisdom of various spiritual traditions and the divine grace that accompanies these virtues.

# Chapter 8

## UNITING IN PURSUING GOODNESS AND LIGHT

In the quest for spiritual freedom, the unifying force of goodness and light serves as a guiding principle across diverse spiritual traditions. It calls upon us to transcend divisions, embrace compassion, and collectively work towards the betterment of humanity.

Let's explore the profound significance of uniting in pursuing goodness and light as a pathway to spiritual liberation.

Goodness represents virtuous and morally upright actions and intentions. It encompasses qualities such as kindness, compassion, honesty, and integrity. Goodness involves seeking the well-being of others and fostering a sense of harmony and justice in the world.

Light symbolizes illumination, truth, and spiritual awakening. Often used metaphorically to represent the divine presence and enlightenment, embracing the light involves seeking spiritual clarity, wisdom, and a deep connection with the divine.

> *"You are the light of the world. A town built on a hill cannot be hidden. Neither do people light a lamp and put it under a bowl. Instead, they put it on its stand, and it gives light to everyone in the house. In the same way, let your light shine before others, that they may see your good deeds and glorify your Father in heaven."*
> — Matthew 5:14-16 (NIV)

This passage from the New Testament emphasizes the connection between light and goodness. It encourages individuals to shine their light through virtuous actions, demonstrating goodness and bringing glory to the divine.

## *Fostering Unity and Harmony*

The pursuit of goodness and light fosters unity and harmony among us and our communities. When people come together to pursue these virtues, they transcend barriers of religion, nationality, and culture, working collectively for the common good.

Goodness and light empower personal transformation, serving as catalysts for inner growth and spiritual awakening. By embodying these qualities, individuals undergo a process of purification and enlightenment, which is central to spiritual freedom.

Goodness and light call upon us to serve others and alleviate suffering. This service is not limited to acts of charity but extends to creating a more just and compassionate society, where all can thrive. Embracing goodness and light deepens one's connection with the divine. It is through these virtues that we draw closer to the source of all goodness and wisdom, experiencing a profound sense of spiritual freedom.

As we embrace the concept of uniting to pursue goodness and light, we realize it is a transformative path to spiritual freedom. It involves breaking free from the constraints of ego, fostering unity and harmony, empowering personal transformation, serving others, and deepening our connection with the divine. The wisdom of various spiritual traditions and scriptural references underscores the profound significance of these virtues in the context of spiritual liberation. As we and communities come together to embrace goodness and light, we contribute to a world filled with compassion, wisdom, and spiritual freedom—a world where the radiant light of goodness dispels the darkness of ignorance and suffering.

## Connecting With the Divine

Embracing goodness and light deepens one's connection with the divine. It is through these virtues that we draw closer to the source of all goodness and wisdom, experiencing a profound sense of spiritual freedom. Connecting with the Divine involves establishing a sacred and intimate relationship with God. It transcends intellectual belief and enters the realm of direct experience and communion with the divine source. Often considered the ultimate source of spiritual freedom, this connection offers us a sense of purpose, guidance, and inner peace.

*"That all of them may be one, Father, just as you are in me and I am in you. May they also be in us so that the world may believe that you have sent me."*
— John 17:21 (NIV)

This verse from the Gospel of John highlights the concept of unity and oneness with the Divine. It emphasizes that we can be in communion with the Divine presence, echoing the idea of connectedness as a path to spiritual freedom.

The Divine connection serves as a source of guidance and purpose. It offers clarity, wisdom, and a sense of direction in life. Being connected with the Divine, we often feel a deep resonance with our life's purpose and mission. The communion with the Divine brings inner peace and fulfillment, offering solace during life's challenges and a profound sense of contentment. This inner peace is a hallmark of spiritual freedom. Connecting with the Divine breaks down the barriers of separation, fostering a sense of oneness with all of creation.

At the heart of many spiritual traditions is the idea of connecting with the Divine. It transcends religious boundaries and offers profound benefits that enhance our overall well-being and sense of purpose.

Connecting with the Divine provides us with spiritual guidance. It offers clarity and direction in life, helping us navigate the complexities of our journey. We receive this guidance through prayer, meditation, or seeking a deeper understanding of the divine presence within and around us.

The communion with the Divine brings inner peace and fulfillment. It allows us to find solace in times of turmoil and contentment in moments of stillness. This inner peace becomes a source of strength, helping us navigate life's challenges.

Connecting with the Divine lies at the heart of spiritual freedom. It transcends religious boundaries and is a universal aspiration shared by seekers across the world. This profound connection liberates us from the limitations of the ego, offers guidance and purpose, brings inner peace and fulfillment, and fosters a sense of oneness with all creation.

As we embark on our spiritual journeys, may we seek to deepen our connection with the Divine, knowing that it is the key to true spiritual freedom that transcends the material world and leads us to the boundless realm of the divine presence.

## *Purpose and Mission*

The Divine connection reveals our life's purpose and mission. It aligns us with a greater sense of calling and empowers us to make meaningful contributions to the world. This sense of purpose gives our lives deep meaning and direction.

*"For I know the plans I have for you, declares the LORD, plans for welfare and not for evil, to give you a future and a hope."*
— Jeremiah 29:11 (NIV)

This well-known verse from the Book of Jeremiah reminds us that the Divine has a specific plan for each of us. It assures us that our purpose aligns with the greater good, providing hope and direction.

Discovering your spiritual purpose and mission is a profound journey guided by the wisdom of the Bible, reminding us we are part of a greater plan, designed to contribute positively to the world. By aligning with our purpose and embracing our mission, we find fulfillment, meaning, and a deeper connection to the Divine. As we navigate this path, let us draw inspiration from the biblical teachings and the assurance that our purpose is a divine gift waiting to be uncovered.

# Chapter 9

## LIVING WITH INTEGRITY

L iving with integrity is a profound and essential aspect of spiritual freedom. It is a concept deeply rooted in various religious and spiritual traditions, emphasizing honesty, moral uprightness, and alignment with one's values and beliefs. Integrity, in its essence, refers to the quality of being honest and having strong moral principles. It involves consistency between one's thoughts, words, and actions. Many spiritual traditions view integrity as a fundamental virtue that leads to inner peace, spiritual growth, and a harmonious existence with oneself and the world.

*"Let your 'Yes' be 'Yes' and your 'No' be 'No.' Anything more than this comes from the evil one"*
—Matthew 5:37(NIV)

This well-known verse reminds us of the need for straightforwardness and truthfulness in one's speech and actions. Living with integrity means being truthful and keeping one's commitments, which align with the core values of Christianity.

The foundation of spiritual freedom is living with integrity. Spiritual freedom is a state of inner liberation, where one is free from the constraints of ego, material desires, and external influences. It is about experiencing a profound connection with the Divine, transcending the limitations of the physical world, and finding peace and purpose in life. Living with integrity is intrinsically linked to spiritual freedom in several ways:

- Living with integrity involves aligning one's actions with higher moral and ethical principles. This alignment brings us closer to the truth and allows us to experience the freedom that comes with inner harmony and authenticity.

   At its core, alignment with higher truth is about seeking and embodying wisdom, compassion, and ethical conduct in one's life. It entails a commitment to living according to principles that promote the well-being of oneself and others, as well as a recognition of a deeper, underlying reality that connects all living beings.

Moreover, alignment with higher truth fosters a sense of inner peace and contentment. When we act according to our deeply held principles, we experience a profound sense of harmony within ourselves. This inner peace allows us to navigate life's challenges with resilience and grace.

In Christianity, the teachings of Jesus emphasize love, forgiveness, and righteousness as principles that lead to alignment with the divine truth. Alignment with higher truth is a universal and transformative concept that transcends religious and spiritual boundaries. It involves living in harmony with principles of wisdom, compassion, and ethical conduct.

This alignment brings inner peace, purpose, and a deeper connection to the fundamental truths that underlie the human experience, making it a vital aspect of the spiritual journey for all of us.

- When we live with integrity, we do not carry the burden of guilt or regret for dishonesty or unethical behavior. This freedom from inner turmoil allows for a deeper connection with one's spiritual self and a sense of purity.

Embracing the idea that mistakes and regrets can serve as opportunities for learning and personal growth is essential. Rather than dwelling on past errors, we can use them as stepping stones toward self-improvement and a deeper understanding of ourselves.

Freedom from guilt and regret is not about denying responsibility for one's actions or disregarding the consequences of past choices. Instead, it is about acknowledging these aspects while reframing them in a way that promotes self-compassion, growth, and a positive outlook on the future.

In many spiritual traditions, the concept of forgiveness plays a central role in achieving freedom from guilt and regret. For instance, Christianity emphasizes forgiveness as a way to release the burden of sin and find redemption. These traditions teach that forgiving oneself and others is a transformative act that leads to spiritual and emotional freedom.

Freedom from guilt and regret is a powerful and liberating state of being. It involves self-forgiveness, learning and growth, living in the present, making amends when necessary, and seeking support when needed. This journey toward emotional healing and liberation is essential for us to move forward in life with a sense of purpose, self-acceptance, and inner peace.

• Integrity fosters trust in relationships, both with oneself and with others. Trust is a fundamental element of spiritual freedom, as it enables open and honest connections with others and with God. Trust and connection hold profound spiritual significance, transcending mere interpersonal dynamics to encompass a deeper, more profound relationship with the self, others, and God.

In the realm of spirituality, trust and connection weave together and play a pivotal role in our journey toward inner peace, purpose, and a sense of belonging. Trust and connection hold profound spiritual significance, transcending mere interpersonal dynamics to encompass a deeper, more profound relationship with oneself, others, and the Divine. Many spiritual traditions emphasize trust in the Divine as a cornerstone of faith, which is rooted in the belief that there is a benevolent force guiding and supporting us in our life's journey. It provides a sense of security, knowing that one is not alone in facing life's challenges. In Christianity, for example, trust in God's plan and providence is fundamental. Spiritual growth often involves developing trust in one's inner wisdom and intuition. It's about recognizing that within each of us resides a divine spark or a higher self that can guide and inspire. Trusting in God is essential for making authentic choices aligned with one's spiritual path.

*Building spiritual connections with others relies on trust, compassion, and empathy.* duplication

Building spiritual connections with others relies on trust, compassion, and empathy. It involves seeing the divine essence in all beings and cultivating a sense of interconnectedness. Spirituality often involves faith in the journey of life itself.

Trusting every experience, whether joyous or challenging, is part of a larger spiritual journey and can provide solace and meaning. This concept teaches how our actions are part of our spiritual journey, and trust in this cosmic process is encouraged.

Trust and connection spiritually lead to a sense of inner peace, harmony, and purpose. They help us navigate life's challenges with resilience and grace. Moreover, they foster a deep sense of belonging, both within oneself and in the broader universe. Whether through faith in God, trust in one's inner guidance (the Holy Spirit) or the recognition of interconnectedness, trust, and connection are transformative forces that elevate the spiritual journey, offering a profound sense of meaning and fulfillment.

- Living with integrity leads to inner peace, which is a cornerstone of spiritual freedom. When one's actions and beliefs are in harmony, there is a profound sense of tranquility and contentment.

    Inner peace is a sacred and transformative state of being, closely intertwined with the concept of spiritual freedom. It represents a profound sense of tranquility, harmony, and contentment that arises from aligning with one's spiritual values, purpose, and a deep understanding of oneself and the world. Inner peace involves liberation from the turbulence of negative emotions, such as anger, fear, and anxiety. Achieving inner peace allows us to transcend these conflicts, providing a sense of calm and serenity. In spiritual traditions, inner peace is often associated with the cessation of suffering, which is considered the ultimate form of spiritual freedom.

Many spiritual paths teach that inner peace arises from a deep connection with God. In Christianity, for example, it's believed that inner peace is a gift from God, and through faith and trust in his plan, one can experience spiritual freedom and tranquility. Inner peace often requires letting go of attachments to material possessions, ego-driven desires, and external validation. This detachment is essential for achieving spiritual freedom, as it shifts the focus from worldly pursuits to inner fulfillment.

Practices like mindfulness and meditation are instrumental in cultivating inner peace. By being fully present in the moment and letting go of the past and dwelling not on the future, we can experience a deep sense of inner calm and spiritual freedom. Inner peace arises when we align with our life's purpose and values. It's about living authentically and according to our spiritual principles. This alignment brings a profound sense of fulfillment and freedom from the inner conflict that arises when our actions contradict our values.

The ability to forgive oneself and others is a crucial component of inner peace and spiritual freedom. Forgiveness allows us to release the burden of past grievances and experience a profound sense of liberation. In essence, inner peace is both a precursor to and a result of spiritual freedom. It serves as a foundation upon which we can build a deeper connection between ourselves and God.

As we journey toward spiritual freedom, we often discover that inner peace is not merely the absence of conflict, but a state of profound serenity and contentment. It is the realization that we are free from the shackles of ego, attachments, and the relentless pursuit of external validation, and instead find solace in the truth of our spiritual essence. In this state, we experience the freedom to live authentically, guided by inner wisdom and purpose, unburdened by the turbulence of the external world. Inner peace, inextricably linked with spiritual freedom, is a state of profound liberation, fulfillment, and harmony that transcends the boundaries of time and circumstance.

• Integrity is closely linked to authenticity, which is a key aspect of spiritual freedom. Authentic living involves being true to oneself and one's values, allowing for a deeper connection with one's spiritual path. Authenticity is a foundational and transformative aspect of spiritual freedom. It involves being true to ourselves, embracing our unique essence, and living in alignment with our deepest values and beliefs. This authenticity is not a superficial adherence to societal norms or expectations, but a profound expression of our inner truth. Authenticity requires us to explore and understand our inner selves deeply. It involves a journey of self-discovery, where we seek to uncover our core values, beliefs, and desires. This alignment with our inner truth is a fundamental step towards spiritual freedom because it enables us to live in harmony with our authentic selves.

Inauthentic living often stems from trying to meet external expectations, whether from society, family, or peers. Spiritual freedom is about breaking free from these external constraints and choosing to live according to our internal compass. By embracing authenticity, we liberate ourselves from the pressure to conform and find the courage to be our true selves.

Authentic living fosters a deep sense of inner peace and fulfillment. When we are authentic, there is no inner conflict between our actions and our true selves. This inner harmony leads to a profound sense of contentment and emotional well-being, which are essential components of spiritual freedom.

Authenticity in relationships is crucial for spiritual freedom. Authentic individuals are open, honest, and vulnerable, which fosters genuine connections with others. These authentic connections provide a sense of belonging and support on the spiritual journey.

Authentic living often leads to a clearer sense of life's purpose. When we are in touch with our true selves, we are better equipped to discern our calling and follow a path that is in alignment with our spiritual goals. This sense of purpose is a driving force behind spiritual freedom.

Authenticity encourages us to accept and love ourselves as we are, flaws and all. Self-acceptance is a powerful step toward spiritual freedom because it liberates us from self-judgment and self-criticism.

The fact of it is authenticity is a central and transformative factor in achieving spiritual freedom. It liberates us from the shackles of conformity, external expectations, and ego-driven motivations. Authentic living fosters inner peace, fulfillment, and genuine connections with others, all of which are essential components of the spiritual journey. Ultimately, spiritual freedom is about finding liberation within ourselves, and authenticity is the key that unlocks the door to that inner liberation. It empowers us to live a life that is true to our deepest essence, values, and purpose, leading to a profound sense of freedom and fulfillment on our spiritual path.

• Living with integrity often means valuing spiritual principles over material gain. This detachment from materialism is a crucial step toward spiritual freedom, as it reduces the attachment to worldly desires.

One of the central tenets of integrity is honesty and truthfulness. This principle is foundational in many spiritual traditions, emphasizing the importance of speaking and living in truth. When we value this spiritual principle over material gains, we choose to be honest in our dealings, even when dishonesty might bring financial rewards. This commitment to truth builds trust in relationships and fosters inner peace, contributing to our spiritual growth.

Spiritual principles often include compassion and altruism, which promote concern for the well-being of others. When we prioritize these principles, we willingly share our resources and help those in need, even at the expense of accumulating material wealth. Compassion-driven actions not only benefit others but also lead to a deep sense of fulfillment and spiritual contentment.

Many spiritual paths advocate for detachment from material possessions. Prioritizing spiritual principles over material gains involves recognizing that pursuing material wealth alone can lead to attachment, greed, and discontent. By cultivating detachment, we free ourselves from the constant craving for more and discover a sense of spiritual freedom and contentment.

Integrity often requires us to champion justice and fairness, even when it challenges our financial interests. Advocating for equitable treatment and standing up against injustice is a core principle in various spiritual and ethical systems. This commitment to fairness aligns with the values of justice and righteousness, fostering a sense of moral fulfillment and spiritual well-being.

Spiritual principles often promote the virtues of generosity and sharing. When we prioritize these principles, we willingly share our resources with others, understanding that our wealth is not solely for personal accumulation but for the greater good. This practice of generosity fosters a sense of interconnectedness and abundance, which are central to spiritual growth.

Some spiritual principles include the responsibility to care for the environment and the Earth. Valuing these principles requires us to make choices that prioritize the well-being of the planet over short-term material gains. This environmental stewardship is seen as an expression of gratitude for the natural world and contributes to a sense of spiritual connectedness.

Prioritizing spiritual principles over material gains often leads to a profound sense of contentment and inner peace. This contentment arises from knowing that our actions are in alignment with our deepest values and beliefs, regardless of external circumstances. It transcends the fleeting happiness derived from material possessions.

Ultimately, living with integrity and valuing spiritual principles over material gains is a path to spiritual growth and fulfillment. It leads us to a deeper understanding of ourselves and our place in the world, fostering a sense of purpose, meaning, and inner richness that transcends the pursuit of material wealth.

It's important to note that valuing spiritual principles over material gains doesn't necessarily mean renouncing wealth or living in poverty. It means making conscious choices that prioritize ethics, compassion, honesty, and justice in all aspects of life, including financial matters. We can use our material resources as tools for positive change, whether through philanthropy, responsible business practices, or simply by leading an ethical and compassionate life.

Living with integrity by valuing spiritual principles over material gains is a transformative and deeply fulfilling way of life. It involves making choices that prioritize honesty, compassion, justice, and ethical conduct, even in the face of financial temptations. This commitment to spiritual values leads to a sense of inner peace, contentment, and fulfillment that transcends the pursuit of material wealth, enriching both our lives and the world around us.

Living with integrity is a vital component of spiritual freedom. It is a virtue celebrated in religious and spiritual traditions, intrinsically linking to inner peace, authenticity, and alignment with higher principles. As the scriptures teach, integrity is a path to spiritual growth, liberation from suffering, and a deeper connection with God. By embodying integrity in our daily lives, we move closer to the spiritual freedom that is at the core of our human existence.

# Chapter 10

## IT'S TIME TO EMBRACE OUR
## SPIRITUALITY WITH BOLDNESS

*"You don't have to be great to start, but you
have to start to be great."*
—Zig Ziglar

Zig Ziglar's statement carries profound wisdom that extends far beyond the realm of personal development and achievement. It has a powerful resonance in the context of spiritual freedom, as it underscores the idea that embarking on a spiritual journey requires a first step, regardless of where we currently stand in our spiritual understanding or practice. In many spiritual and religious traditions, pursuing spiritual growth is a central tenet. It is said that human beings have the potential for spiritual greatness, but it is not inherent. Instead, it requires a deliberate and often arduous effort to attain.

*"Ask and it will be given to you; seek, and you will find; knock, and it will be open to you."*
—Matthew 7:7

This passage emphasizes the importance of seeking spiritual understanding and growth. It implies that one must start their spiritual journey with the act of seeking and asking.

*"I press on toward the goal for the prize of the upward call of God in Christ Jesus."*
—Philippians 3:14

This verse underscores the idea that spiritual growth is a continuous process that requires effort and perseverance. It reinforces the notion that one doesn't need to be spiritually perfect from the outset, but must begin the journey and persistently press forward.

## *The Transformational Power of Starting*

In pursuing spiritual freedom, one of the most potent catalysts is the simple act of starting. It is the willingness to embark on a journey of self-discovery and transformation, to take the first step on a path that leads to profound spiritual growth. Starting, in the context of spirituality, is about breaking free from inertia, complacency, and the constraints of the past to unleash the transformative power that resides within all of us.

The transformational power of starting is a fundamental concept that underscores the capacity of us to effect a profound change in our lives and the world at large by taking that initial step towards a goal or aspiration. At its core, starting represents the spark of action, the ignition of potential, and the birth of progress. It is the moment when intention transforms into reality, and dreams materialize, forever altering lives.

To understand the significance of starting, we must first recognize its universal applicability. Regardless of age, gender, background, or circumstance, everyone has the power to start something. Whether it's embarking on a new career path, launching a business, or pursuing your life's purpose, the act of starting is the common denominator for all accomplishments. It embodies the human spirit's innate drive for growth, learning, and improvement.

Starting is the antidote to inertia and complacency. It propels us out of our comfort zones and into the realm of growth and progress. It challenges us to confront our fears, uncertainties, and doubts. It encourages us to embrace the unknown, where transformation thrives. The act of starting always involves a risk that we find the greatest potential for personal and societal growth. To start is to acknowledge the possibility of failure, but also the prospect of success.

The transformational power of starting is a force that propels us, communities, and societies forward. It is the spark of action, the birth of progress, and the catalyst for change. The act of starting embodies our innate capacity for growth and transformation, and it is a testament to human potential. It is through starting that we overcome inertia, confront challenges, and achieve our goals. It is through starting that we leave a mark on the world and inspire others to do the same.

In this act of initiation, we find the power to create, to innovate, to connect, and to transform our lives and the world around us. As we embrace the transformational power of starting, we release the past, transcend the limitations of the ego, and open ourselves to the infinite possibilities of spiritual growth. Each step we take is a step towards spiritual freedom, and each beginning is an opportunity to experience the profound and liberating transformation of the soul.

# Conclusion

In the quest for spiritual freedom and the unveiling of the soul, we embark on a journey that transcends the boundaries of the material world, seeking a profound connection with the divine.

As we journey into the depths of our spiritual selves, we discover that there is indeed a difference between those who seek to know God and those who do not. This journey leads us to a place of greater self-awareness, humility, and inner peace. It teaches us to embrace the transformative power of starting, breaking free from inertia and fear, and committing to a path of continuous self-improvement and spiritual growth. It encourages us to overcome the limitations of the ego, acknowledge our imperfections, and cultivate compassion, love, and wisdom.

In contrast, those who have not embarked on this spiritual journey may remain confined by the constraints of materialism, ego, and pursuing worldly desires. They may find themselves bound by the fear of the unknown and disconnected from the deeper dimensions of existence.

What distinguishes those who seek to know God from those who do not is their willingness to explore the uncharted territories of the soul, to acknowledge the existence of something greater than ourselves, and to commit to a life of spiritual growth and self-realization. It is a journey that sets us on a path to spiritual freedom, where we unveil the soul and experience a profound and liberating transformation.

In our pursuit of spiritual freedom and the unveiling of the soul, let us remember the importance of this journey and the difference it makes in our lives. It is a path that leads to a deeper understanding of ourselves, a connection with the divine, and a life imbued with purpose, compassion, and inner peace.

May we continue to embrace this journey with open hearts, knowing that in doing so, we set ourselves apart in our quest to know God and discover the true essence of our spiritual selves.

## Conclusion

In *Unveiling the Soul,* readers will gain a deeper understanding of hesitations that arise within us on our journeys. By addressing these challenges head-on, we can unlock our true spiritual potential and live a more authentic life. This book encourages believers to embrace our spirituality, express it confidently, and nurture our unique connection with the divine.

*"Go therefore and make disciples of all nations, baptizing them in the name of the Father and of the Son and of the Holy Spirit, teaching them to observe all that I have commanded you."*
— Matthew 28:19-20 (NIV)

Known as the Great Commission, these words of Jesus in the Gospel of Matthew underscore our mission as followers of Christ. It is a call to spread love, knowledge, and transformation to all corners of the world.

# About the Author

Meet Robert E Smith, a multifaceted individual whose life story weaves a narrative of faith, purpose, and transformation. Hailing from Belize City, Belize, Robert discovered his divine calling at a young age, sensing that the Lord had set him apart for a specific purpose.

A minister and a licensed contractor, Robert's journey unfolds with rich experiences that shape his character and convictions. In his debut book, "If Not Now, Then When? Unveiling the Soul in Search of Spiritual Freedom," he eloquently explores the depths of the human spirit and the pursuit of true liberation.

Robert's professional path took him through a decade-long career as an office space designer before venturing into the realm of construction, where his expertise as a sought-after builder became widely recognized. Despite the demands of his secular pursuits, he remained dedicated to his spiritual calling, teaching Bible study and Sunday school throughout his journey.

Known for his unwavering commitment to truth and integrity, Robert, often referred to as a pastor due to his strong moral character, initially resisted the idea of becoming a working pastor. However, two years before retirement, he embraced his divine calling to serve in the field of ministry.

Robert E Smith's influence extends beyond construction sites; he is a beacon of spiritual wisdom and a masterful biblical teacher. His goal is clear—to empower individuals to make conscious and informed decisions about pursuing their spiritual freedom. Through his life's work and written words, Robert inspires others to embark on their own journeys of self-discovery, faith, and purpose, leaving an indelible mark on those fortunate enough to cross paths with this remarkable minister and author.

www.ingramcontent.com/pod-product-compliance
Lightning Source LLC
Chambersburg PA
CBHW020329130626
46549CB00003B/1082